GET TO THE ROOT OF IT
A guide to emotional Healing

Scripture passages taken from

The Holy Bible, New King James Version (NKJV) Copyright © 1982 and New Spirit-Filled Life © Bible 2002 unless otherwise indicated.

All definitions taken from the Merriam–Webster's Collegiate Dictionary, Eleventh Edition. Copyright © 2003 Merriam-Webster incorporated.

BIBLICAL DELIVERANCE

We are acutely aware that God is the healer, and man is a conduit through which the healing power of God flows. In many passages in the Gospel, Jesus freed people from demonic oppression. The Bible uses the term *salvation* (Romans 1:16), which means "deliverance, liberation, or rescue." The word *deliver* literally means to "set free."

When I asked God years ago, "Why did the children of Israel keep going back into bondage?" He said, "Because they never drove out all of the enemies."

You can be spiritually advancing and remain emotionally crippled. What you fail to kill will ultimately kill you. A weakness ignored can only increase; not dealing with it gives it permission to grow. God has given us power over the power of Satan, and he can't do anything without our permission.

Deliverance is an act; healing is a process. *Deliverance* is "the act by which the Spirit of God, with your permission, confronts demonic power, exerts His authority, and removes Satan from the premises." *Healing* is "the process by which you and the Spirit of God begin repairing the effects of demonic activity and sin." For example, if your house is infested by termites and the exterminator comes but the effects of termite infestation remain, this is similar to deliverance. The enemy is gone, but the residue and damage remains. The effects of demonic oppression take place in your soul, and that is why the Word says, "Satan is the enemy of our souls" (Psalm 143:3).

God wants us to prosper as our souls prosper. The prosperity of the soul determines the longevity, effectiveness, and magnitude with which we maximize our lives and the lives of others. When deliverance and healing are fully manifested, you are no longer led by impulses or demonic coercion; your soul is now subject to your spirit, and you are now free to serve God and build the kingdom free from internal resistance.

GET TO THE ROOT OF IT

"And even now the axe is laid to the root of the trees. Therefore, every tree which does not bear good fruit is cut down and thrown into the fire" (Matthew 3:10).

One of the things I have seen in the lives of many people, believers and unbelievers alike, is the issues that lie dormant in our souls eventually manifest in one of two ways: (1) at the peak of our success, these issues crop up destroying what you spent years working to create, or (2) our root issues are so out of control that we never quite get our life off the ground. We are plagued by condemnation, anxiety, feelings of inadequacy, anger, rejection, and lack of forgiveness. The pain is overshadowed by addictive behaviors, sex, alcohol, drugs, and emotional dysfunction.

A *root* is "anything that is allowed to grow and weave itself around our mind, will, and emotions." Roots are "demonic fortifications," or as the Bible refers to them, *strongholds*. They are created when we allow an emotional trauma to go unopposed. That is why our response to any given situation determines if it will be a passing event or a lifelong struggle. An improper response can take root and then take years to discover let alone destroy. Jesus said, "Agree with your adversary quickly" (Matthew 5:21). "Anything that can hinder our maturity in Christ" is an *adversary*.

These root issues can be intricate and intertwine themselves around every aspect of our lives. They can and will strangle the life out of every relationship and endeavor to hinder our forward progress. These root issues are the things that lie just beneath the surface of our lives, and we spend enormous amounts of money, energy, and time dealing with the fruit that will only continue to grow if the roots are not destroyed. Unfortunately, we spend much of our anointing fixing our issues and mistakes rather than advancing the kingdom. We understand that many childhood traumas were completely beyond our control, but it is never too late to take authority over the Enemy. This is when we rely on the work of the Holy Spirit to reveal these issues.

Many times, in the Bible, Jesus spoke in parables. *Parables* were "natural examples used to explain a spiritual truth" (Mark 4:5-8). Explaining the natural root system of plants provides a visual of how deadly these issues can be. We can pull weeds all day long, but until we dig up the roots, our yard will be covered with weeds again in a matter of weeks. The root systems in plants are intricately designed and driven to make sure the plant they are supporting lives, grows, and thrives.

The sole purpose of the banyan tree or strangler fig is to be an agent of death. The strangler fig seeds take root in the crevice of a host tree, completely taking over the feeding source of the host tree, wrapping its roots around the tree until the host no longer lives or is a mere shadow of what it once was. The same is true of our issues. Satan's driving aim is to maintain the vitality of these negative root issues, making sure they thrive and grow. The root systems for trees can be as deep as the tree is tall. Our prayer for you is that you truly recognize and break free from these agents of death that can strangle the life out of you and leave you a mere shadow of who you are supposed to be.

In my years in ministry, I have seen gifted, anointed, talented people self-destruct time and time again. I believe it can be attributed to one passage in the Bible that is grossly overlooked: "Now when the devil had ended every temptation, he departed from Him until an *opportune time*" (Luke 4:13). Satan is absolutely waiting to ambush us. The Bible says, "Your adversary the devil walks about like a roaring lion, seeking whom he may devour" (1 Peter 5:8).

The effectiveness of 9/11 was because we didn't know the enemy was here. Even though Satan was defeated by God, he must be perpetually defeated by us. Satan being defeated in our lives is directly proportionate to our ability to prohibit fleshly desires from being our guiding compass and letting our faith succumb to the constant barrage of his attacks. These inner issues can so greatly affect the magnitude with which we interact with the world in which we live. We cannot truly change or make change until we acknowledge the flaws in ourselves, especially the ones that we so desperately try to hide. Our moral responsibility is to refuse to be vessels of deception and destruction.

I, too, have experienced the crippling effects of some of these issues. I had to really dig in deep with God and confront these issues. No one is exempt. One preacher said, "No one has a franchise on pain." There is hope, help, and healing if you are willing to travel along the rugged terrain and allow God to bring healing and deliverance like you have never experienced. He is faithful to the saved!

We believe the distinctive keys to deliverance are:

FAITH: "And Jesus answered them, "Have faith in God" (Mark 11:22).

In its purest definition, this verse means we can trust that God is who He says He is and He will do what He says He will do, regardless of what our outward circumstances are dictating. We are commanded in the Word to walk by faith in God—not by what we see or feel.

REPENTENCE: "If we confess our sins, He is faithful and just to forgive us our sins and to cleanse us from all unrighteousness" (1 John 1:9).

True repentance is confessing your sins and not repeating them. The word says we are to bear fruit worthy of repentance. In other words, if we say we have repented, our behavior should be consistent with the confession that our mouths have made.

CONFESSION: "For assuredly, I say to you, whoever says to this mountain, 'Be removed and be cast into the sea,' and does not doubt in his heart, but believes that those things he says will be done, he will have whatever he says" (Mark 11:23).

We are so often "hung by the tongue." We fail to understand that what comes out of our mouth has a significant impact on our lives and the lives of others. It is important to understand that the words we speak matter. Be careful to speak what you want to manifest in your life.

SPIRITUAL SENSITIVITY: "However, when He, the Spirit of truth, has come, He will guide you into all truth; for He will not speak on His own authority, but whatever He hears He will speak; and He will tell you things to come" (John 16:13).

As our teacher and guide, our sensitivity to the voice of the Holy Spirit is paramount. He will always give us instruction concerning what we need to do to maximize our healing.

OBEDIENCE: "As obedient children, not conforming yourselves to the former lusts, as in your ignorance; [15]but as He who called you is holy, you also be holy in all your conduct" (I Peter 1:14-15).

In conjunction with having sensitivity to the Holy Spirit, *obedience* means "doing what He said to do." This is one of the keys to determining how much of our healing will manifest in our life. If the Holy Spirit commands us to change our diet, stop smoking or end a relationship, it is imperative that we follow through.

PRAYER: "Praying always with all prayer and supplication in the Spirit, being watchful to this end with all perseverance and supplication for all the saints" (Ephesians 6:18).

Prayer is "staying in close fellowship with God through verbal communication." It helps us bring the mind and will of God into our lives, knowing that His ultimate will is that we be healed spirit, soul, and body.

CHURCH ATTENDANCE: "Let us hold fast the confession of our hope without wavering, for He who promised is faithful. And let us consider one another in order to stir up love and good works, not forsaking the assembling of ourselves together, as is the manner of some, but exhorting one another, and so much the more as you see the Day approaching" (Hebrews 10:23-25).

Fellowship with the saints of God is more important than most people realize. In this area, the Enemy's goal is to get us out of an environment that can empower us to stay consistent and strong in our Christian walk.

FORGIVENESS: "For if you forgive men their trespasses, your heavenly Father will also forgive you (Matthew 6:14).

True forgiveness toward others and ourselves releases us from the claws of the Enemy. When we forgive, we relinquish our right to retaliate and defend our position. Faith is a spiritual transaction. We may not always feel like we have forgiven, but the more we walk in it, the quicker our emotions will come into alignment with the decision we have made. It is important to understand that forgiveness is a process and does not happen overnight.

Finally, we are praying for you and are so excited about the work that we know the Holy Spirit will do in your life. It is not an easy process but one that is essential for you to fulfill your purpose and destiny in God. We declare that the Holy Spirit will comfort, keep, protect, reveal, and guide you as you cooperate with Him concerning your healing. We love and thank you for giving us the opportunity to minister to you.

DAILY CONFESSION

Heavenly Father, I thank You that, because of the blood of Jesus, we can boldly approach Your throne and obtain mercy when we need it. We enter Your gates with thanksgiving and Your courts with praise. We are thankful unto You and bless Your Holy name. I thank You that You are the only living God, the only wise God, the Holy one of Israel, the God of Abraham, Isaac, and Jacob, Wonderful Counselor, Mighty God, Everlasting Father, Prince of Peace, the Way, the Truth, the Light, the Door, the Bread of Life, the Good Shepherd, the Redeemer, King of kings, Lord of lords, the Alpha and the Omega, the First and the Last, the Beginning and the End, the Lord God, strong and mighty in battle, and the God who is able to keep me from falling.

I renounce in my life all affiliation with rejection, bitterness, resentment, shame, guilt, condemnation, lying, sexual immorality, self-hatred, sickness, disease, witchcraft, sorcery, fear, anger, anxiety, manipulating spirits, depression, worry, suicidal ideations, and every work of the flesh. I close every door in my soul to which the Enemy has had access and seal it with the blood of Jesus. I come against every lie of the Enemy I have believed and declare that I have the mind of Christ and believe God's Word only. I thank You that the blood of Jesus can cleanse my mind from dead works and an evil conscience, and I give the blood permission to work now!

I cancel and speak death to every fruit, root, tentacle, link, and spirit that would hinder me in my forward movement in God. I am no longer bound by the lust of flesh, the lust of the eyes and the pride of life, but I am strong in the Lord and in the power of His might and believe that the greater one lives inside of me. I thank You that by Your stripes I am completely healed.

Lord, I ask that You forgive me for my involvement with the powers of darkness and no longer give them power to operate in my life. Create in me a clean heart and renew a right spirit in me. Restore unto me the joy of my salvation. I release and give the fruit of the Spirit permission to operate within me in love, joy, peace, longsuffering, meekness, kindness, goodness, faithfulness, gentleness, and self-control. I thank You that I don't need to learn anything by tragedy, accidents, mishaps, or lack, but I hear Your voice and will not follow the voice of the stranger. I declare that I am not moved by anything but Your spirit. My family is blessed, my business is blessed, the work of my hands is blessed, and I am taught by the Lord. Great is my peace and undisturbed composure.

I declare that I will speak only what is righteous, holy, and edifying to myself and others. I stand in agreement with the words I have just spoken and declare that the Enemy has no power to retaliate against my loved ones or me.

Table of Contents

REJECTION

"All whom My Father gives to Me will come to Me; and the one who comes to Me I will most certainly not cast out I will never, no never, reject one of them who comes to Me" (John 6:37).

Rejection is "to refuse to accept or consider; to throw back or away; refuse to hear or receive."

Rejection is a very difficult issue to overcome because this emotion counteracts the one basic human need that we all require to thrive—love. The more significant the relationship, the deeper the wound will be. Rejection leaves us in a perpetual state of never quite feeling loved or accepted by people and always feeling we are on the outside looking in. Issues of rejection constantly ravage the relationships that are close and dear to us, often leaving them broken and unproductive.

MANIFESTATIONS

Low self-esteem

Feelings of being unwanted

Fear of abandonment

Addiction (i.e., sex, drugs, self-injury)

Victim mentality (the blame game)

Jealousy and envy

HOW DO I HEAL?

Repent for cooperating with spirit/feelings of rejection.

Accept your life no matter how bad it may have been.

Accept that God truly loves you and wants to heal you.

Accept and believe by faith that you are absolutely forgiven.

Take responsibility for your own emotions and responses.

DAY 1

DAY 2

DAY 3

_____
_____
_____
_____
_____
_____
_____
_____
_____
_____
_____
_____
_____
_____
_____
_____
_____
_____
_____
_____
_____
_____
_____
_____
_____
_____
_____
_____
_____
_____
_____
_____
_____
_____
_____
_____
_____
_____

DAY 4

_____
_____
_____
_____
_____
_____
_____
_____
_____
_____
_____
_____
_____
_____
_____
_____
_____
_____
_____
_____
_____
_____
_____
_____
_____
_____
_____
_____
_____
_____
_____
_____
_____
_____
_____
_____
_____

DAY 5

DAY 6

DAY 7

<u>DAY 8</u>

DAY 9

DAY 10

DAY 11

DAY 12

DAY 13

DAY 14

BITTERNESS AND LACK OF FORGIVENESS

"See to it that no one fail to obtain the grace of God; that no *root of bitterness* spring up and cause trouble, and by it many become defiled…" (Hebrews 12:15).

Bitterness is "an intense unresolved animosity toward an individual."

Bitterness develops from an inappropriate response to grief or maltreatment. If we somehow believe that an event that has transpired could have been prevented, we tend to blame God and the people involved. When bitterness results from maltreatment, we struggle to forgive. Releasing bitterness is relinquishing your right to defend or retaliate, knowing that vengeance comes from the Lord; He will repay. The appropriate response to our enemies is to "bless them." The root of all bitterness comes from a lack of forgiveness. When we forgive, we release people from a penalty and accept that they owe us nothing—no matter what was done to us. Understand that forgiveness is a process that will take time and is not the same as trust. We can forgive someone, but that person will still have to earn back our trust if he or she is to remain in our life.

MANIFESTATIONS

Resentment

Hatred

Loathing

Anger at others and God

Cynical and critical spirit

HOW DO I HEAL?

Repent for cooperating with a spirit of bitterness.

Be willing to release old hurts and wounds.

Develop a heart of forgiveness toward anyone who has hurt you.

Cultivate a heart of forgiveness toward God.

DAY 1

DAY 2

<u>DAY 3</u>

_____
_____
_____
_____
_____
_____
_____
_____
_____
_____
_____
_____
_____
_____
_____
_____
_____
_____
_____
_____
_____
_____
_____
_____
_____
_____
_____
_____
_____
_____
_____
_____
_____
_____
_____
_____
_____
_____
_____
_____

DAY 4

<u>DAY 5</u>

_____
_____
_____
_____
_____
_____
_____
_____
_____
_____
_____
_____
_____
_____
_____
_____
_____
_____
_____
_____
_____
_____
_____
_____
_____
_____
_____
_____
_____
_____
_____
_____
_____
_____
_____
_____
_____

DAY 6

DAY 7

DAY 8

DAY 9

DAY 10

_____
_____
_____
_____
_____
_____
_____
_____
_____
_____
_____
_____
_____
_____
_____
_____
_____
_____
_____
_____
_____
_____
_____
_____
_____
_____
_____
_____
_____
_____
_____
_____
_____
_____
_____
_____
_____
_____

DAY 11

DAY 12

<u>DAY 13</u>

DAY 14

FEAR

"For God has not given us a spirit of fear, but of power and of love, peace and of a sound mind" (2 Timothy 1:7).

Fear is "alarm and agitation caused by expectation or retaliation of danger."

The powerful emotion of fear can become a self-inflicted prison that keeps a person from fulfilling his or her God-given purpose. Fear can totally and completely paralyze a person. Don't let fear dominate your life or you will never accomplish much. Many times, what you fear never even materializes. The very nature of fear is to hinder your forward progress and upward mobility. Being afraid is acceptable, but you **must** press through fear. Being full of fear is something that can linger for a lifetime if you refuse to face and overcome this emotion.

MANIFESTATIONS

Worry

Anxiety

Panic attacks

Night terrors

Phobias

Obsessive compulsive disorders

HOW DO I HEAL?

Repent for cooperating with a spirit of fear.

Renew your mind with the Word of God.

Come against the spirit of fear with the blood of Jesus.

Allow the Lord to love you because you are fully accepted by Him.

DAY 1

<u>DAY 2</u>

DAY 3

DAY 4

DAY 5

DAY 6

DAY 7

DAY 8

DAY 9

DAY 10

DAY 11

_____
_____
_____
_____
_____
_____
_____
_____
_____
_____
_____
_____
_____
_____
_____
_____
_____
_____
_____
_____
_____
_____
_____
_____
_____
_____
_____
_____
_____
_____
_____
_____
_____
_____
_____
_____
_____
_____

<u>DAY 12</u>

_____
_____
_____
_____
_____
_____
_____
_____
_____
_____
_____
_____
_____
_____
_____
_____
_____
_____
_____
_____
_____
_____
_____
_____
_____
_____
_____
_____
_____
_____
_____
_____
_____
_____
_____
_____
_____
_____
_____
_____

DAY 13

DAY 14

GUILT AND CONDEMNATION

"Therefore, there is now no condemnation to those who are in Christ Jesus, who do not walk according to the flesh, but according to the Spirit" (Romans 8:1).

Guilt is "the feeling (realized or believed) that a moral standard or code has been violated."

Generally, the guilt a Christian deal with is false. The Spirit of the Lord does not make us feel guilty or condemn us. His responsibility is to convict us of sin. Conviction leads us to repentance and reconciliation with God. Guilt causes us to feel condemned and unworthy, never feeling like we quite measure up. A religious spirit is the root of false guilt, making us think that we have to be perfect for God to accept us. Jesus said, "Religion kills but the words that I speak are spirit and they are life." The mercy of God assures us that once we have accepted Christ, we are made whole and acceptable by the blood. Our responsibility as a believer is to make sure that we are doing our part to be obedient to God. Guilt, shame and condemnation are strong companions.

MANIFESTATIONS

Shame

Condemnation

Fearing that God is angry at us

Regret

Depression

HOW DO I HEAL?

Repent for cooperating with a spirit of guilt.

Repent of any known sin and strive daily for obedience.

Come against a spirit of religion operating in your life.

Accept that you are acceptable to God because of Christ's sacrifice.

DAY 1

DAY 2

<u>DAY 3</u>

DAY 4

DAY 5

DAY 6

DAY 7

DAY 8

DAY 9

DAY 10

DAY 11

DAY 12

DAY 13

DAY 14

ABUSE

"Let all bitterness, wrath, anger, clamor, and evil speaking be put away from you, with all malice. And be kind to one another, tenderhearted…" (Ephesians 4:31, 32).

Abuse is "the inappropriate or excessive use or treatment; misuse."

Abuse can take many forms, including spiritual, verbal, sexual, physical and emotional. We **must be very clear about the Bible's condemnation of violence and abuse. More than one hundred Biblical passages addressing battering, violence, rape, incest, stalking, lying in wait, twisting the words of another, threats, and intimidation. Since the Word of God condemns violence and abuse, the church must as well.** The effects of abuse, which can be devastating, are designed to reduce and diminish a person's self-worth and self-esteem. Abuse is a means people use to control others. Submission is not a license to abuse; rather, submitting is supposed to give the one submitting an advantage. If you are being abused in any way, we encourage you to seek professional help and remove yourself, if necessary.

MANIFESTATIONS

Fear

Addictions

Anger

Low self-esteem

Depression

HOW DO I HEAL?

Seek professional help.

If you are in an abusive relationship, seek the Lord for Wisdom.

Come against the spirit of fear with the blood of Jesus.

DAY 1

DAY 2

DAY 3

DAY 4

DAY 5

<u>DAY 6</u>

DAY 7

<u>DAY 8</u>

DAY 9

DAY 10

DAY 11

DAY 12

DAY 13

DAY 14

SEXUAL SINS AND SOUL TIES

"…Sexual immorality and all uncleanness or covetousness, let it not even be named among you, as is fitting for saints…" (Ephesians 5:3).

Sexual sin is "any act of intimate contact outside of biblical boundaries." The most common sexual sins include adultery, fornication, masturbation, homosexuality and engaging in pornography. A *soul tie* is "a spiritual attachment to an individual, which can be healthy or unhealthy; the strongest of which are created through illicit sexual activity." Unless these soul ties are severed, they will continue to do damage to our souls and our relationships and can go undetected for years.

Sexual sins are silent killers. Most people do not understand the damage that sexual sin does to their soul. Sexual sin occurs when we allow improper sexual drives to control us. Sex is also a tool used to fulfill our unmet emotional needs. Many of those in sexual sin desire to be spiritual but become enslaved to internal sensual desires that drive them into sin. The Bible says we are to vehemently come against the "lust of the flesh and the lust of the eyes." Sexual sin is devastating to all parties involved and wreaks havoc on a person's spiritual health.

MANIFESTATIONS

Sexual addiction

Children born out of wedlock

Venereal diseases and STDs

Negative soul ties

HOW DO I HEAL?

Repent for being involved in sexual sin.

Allow the Spirit of God by His Word to purify you again.

Renew your mind to the Word of God regarding purity.

Come against the lust of the flesh and the lust of the eyes.

DAY 1

<u>DAY 2</u>

_____
_____
_____
_____
_____
_____
_____
_____
_____
_____
_____
_____
_____
_____
_____
_____
_____
_____
_____
_____
_____
_____
_____
_____
_____
_____
_____
_____
_____
_____
_____
_____
_____
_____
_____
_____
_____

<u>DAY 3</u>

DAY 4

DAY 5

DAY 6

<u>DAY 7</u>

DAY 8

DAY 9

DAY 10

DAY 11

DAY 12

DAY 13

DAY 14

www.ingramcontent.com/pod-product-compliance
Lightning Source LLC
Chambersburg PA
CBHW071904090426
42811CB00004B/741